RAND 1700 Main Street, PO Box 2138 Santa Monica, CA 90407-2138

ERRATA

November 25, 2002

PUBLICATIONS
DEPARTMENT

To: Recipients of *A Preliminary Analysis of Advance
        Appropriations as a Budgeting Method for Navy Ship
        Procurements*, by Irv Blickstein, and Giles Smith
        (MR-1527-NAVY)

From: Publications Department

A key source was omitted, as follows:

The first paragraph on page 6 paraphrases Ronald O'Rourke and Stephen Daggett, *Defense Procurement: Full Funding Policy— Background, Issues, and Options for Congress*, Congressional Research Service, May 7, 2002.

The material on advance appropriations on page 7 is also informed by O'Rourke and Daggett.

T0159562

A Preliminary Analysis of ADVANCE APPROPRIATIONS as a Budgeting Method for Navy Ship Procurements

Irv Blickstein · Giles Smith

Approved for public release; distribution unlimited
Prepared for the United States Navy

RAND

National Defense Research Institute

The research described in this report was conducted for the U.S. Navy within the Acquisition and Technology Policy Center of RAND's National Defense Research Institute, a federally funded research and development center supported by the Office of the Secretary of Defense, the Joint Staff, the unified commands, and the defense agencies under Contract DASW01-01-C-0004.

Library of Congress Cataloging-in-Publication Data

Blickstein, Irv, 1939–
    A preliminary analysis of advance appropriations as a budgeting method for
Navy ship procurements / Irv Blickstein, Giles K. Smith.
      p. cm.
    "MR-1527."
    Includes bibliographical references.
    ISBN 0-8330-3170-8
    1. United States. Navy—Appropriations and expenditures. 2. Warships—United
States. I. Smith, Giles K., 1928– II.Title.

VA60 .B58 2002
359.6'212—dc21

                                           2002067904

Cover: U.S. Navy photo provided without endorsement expressed or implied.

RAND is a nonprofit institution that helps improve policy and decisionmaking through research and analysis. RAND® is a registered trademark. RAND's publications do not necessarily reflect the opinions or policies of its research sponsors.

Cover design by Maritta Tapanainen

© Copyright 2002 RAND

All rights reserved. No part of this book may be reproduced in any form by any electronic or mechanical means (including photocopying, recording, or information storage and retrieval) without permission in writing from RAND.

Published 2002 by RAND
1700 Main Street, P.O. Box 2138, Santa Monica, CA 90407-2138
1200 South Hayes Street, Arlington, VA 22202-5050
201 North Craig Street, Suite 202, Pittsburgh, PA 15213-1516
RAND URL: http://www.rand.org/
To order RAND documents or to obtain additional information,
contact Distribution Services: Telephone: (310) 451-7002;
Fax: (310) 451-6915; Email: order@rand.org

The Navy shipbuilding program typically comprises a few individually very expensive projects, together with an irregular schedule of new starts. Such a combination can lead to major fluctuations in year-to-year budget totals, even when everything proceeds according to a long-range plan. However, major defense acquisition programs rarely exhibit long-term stability: Changing circumstances dictate changing needs; programs run into problems, causing both schedule and cost overruns; etc. Furthermore, when the Navy prepares its budget, the relatively large shipbuilding portion is occasionally used as a source of funds to meet other needs. The resulting fluctuations in an account as large as shipbuilding (it is usually about 10 percent of the Navy's budget), combined with a budget cycle that normally requires major allocation decisions to be made two to three years before the appropriation year, can pose major problems.

The Program Executive Office for Carriers, Naval Sea Systems Command, asked RAND to objectively assess the advantages and disadvantages of the current full-funding policy for aircraft carriers in comparison with those of other funding strategies, including incremental funding and the creation of a revolving fund:

> John Birkler, John F. Schank, James Chiesa, Giles Smith, Irv Blickstein, Ronald D. Fricker, Jr., and Denis Rushworth, *Options for Funding Aircraft Carriers*, Santa Monica, Calif.: RAND, MR-1526-NAVY, 2002.

Subsequently, the Deputy Chief of Naval Operations (N8, Resources, Requirements and Assessments) asked RAND to conduct a similar study that examined the pros and cons of advance appropriations, with possible application across a broader segment of the Navy ship-building program. This report presents results of the analysis of advance appropriations and how it might be employed in funding future ship-acquisition programs. It should be of interest to those in the Navy, Department of Defense, Office of the Secretary of Defense, and Congress involved in budgeting for ships.

This research was sponsored by the Deputy Chief of Naval Operations (N8, Resources, Requirements and Assessments). It was conducted by the Acquisition and Technology Policy Center of RAND's National Defense Research Institute, a federally funded research and development center sponsored by the Office of the Secretary of Defense, the Joint Staff, the unified commands, and the defense agencies.

CONTENTS

TABLES

1. To only one ship at a time (for example, an aircraft carrier, which is started only once every few years and incurs a large one-time cost)

2. To one class of ships (submarines, for example)

3. To some other combination of projects, with the application shifting over time as circumstances dictate

4. To the entire Navy shipbuilding program.

Likewise, varied results can be achieved through use of advance appropriations, depending on the particular application and the circumstances prevailing at the time. Three types of results, or consequences, seem most important:

1. Less year-to-year fluctuation in the overall agency budget. The budget for the projects, as well as the expenditures for it, are spread over several years instead of occurring all in the initial budget year. This smoothing process will incur *increases* in budget totals for some years to balance the *decreases* achieved in other years.

2. A one-time "perceived budget surplus": By deferring to later years part of the budget that would have been appropriated in a particular year, the overall budget totals for the initial year of a project are reduced. This perceived surplus represents the difference between the total budget that would have been required under classical full funding and the budget required under advance appropriations, *in the initial year of a project.* Such funds are not *saved*, they are only *deferred* to some future years.

   Think of this perceived surplus from advance appropriations as purchasing an item by paying part of the price in cash and charging the remainder to a credit card. The deferred charges must be paid in future periods, but as the credit-card balance is paid down, additional items can be purchased and charged against the card. Thus, the original credit-card debt can be renewed indefinitely and can be treated as a one-time fund that the buyer could use for other purposes. In the same way, use of advance appropriations moves some of the appropriations for a program to future years, and the amount deferred could be used to cover exceptional, *one-time* costs in some other program without requiring an increase in the total budget *for that year,* provided that Congress and other government agencies approved of such use.

3. Constraint on the flexibility of management to cope with future unprogrammed events, especially events such as a budget cut that requires a reduction in new-construction starts. Widespread application of advance appropriations causes some portion of each year's funds to be spent paying the deferred elements of programs started in prior years. Thus, only a portion of the total budget in any year is available to absorb any reduction in overall budget that might be imposed. Returning to the credit-card analogy, if the borrower suffers a reduction in income, that reduction will be imposed entirely on the borrower's funds remaining *after* making the credit-card payments for that period.

The application of advance appropriations to the Shipbuilding and Conversion–Navy (SCN) budget would represent a major change in budget-management strategy, posing both opportunities and risks. The balance of those consequences will be perceived differently at different times and from different institutional perspectives. We made an initial exploration of some of the implementation issues that might be encountered. We found no compelling balance of such considerations, either for or against such a strategy.

ACKNOWLEDGMENTS

This work could not have been undertaken without the steadfast support and encouragement we received from Vice Admiral Edmund P. Giambastiani, Jr., U.S. Navy, and Dr. Susan Marquis, then the Deputy and Assistant Deputy Chief of Naval Operations (Resources, Warfare Requirements and Assessments), respectively, and their staff, who graciously provided many of the data necessary and patiently answered our many questions.

For their careful and constructive comments on earlier drafts, we thank RAND colleagues Frank Lacroix and Frank Camm. We are also indebted to Joan Myers for her deft assistance in organizing and formatting the many drafts and to Marian Branch for her editing.

AA	Advance appropriations
AKE	Auxiliary Cargo and Ammunition ship
AP	Advance procurement
CNO	Chief of Naval Operations
CVN	Carrier vessel, nuclear
CVNX	Carrier vessel, nuclear, new design
DD	Destroyer
DDG	Destroyer, guided-missile
JCC	Joint Command and Control ship
LHD	Amphibious assault ship (multipurpose)
LPD	Landing Platform–Dock
LSD	Dock Landing Ship
MYP	Multiyear procurements
OMB	Office of Management and Budget
OSD	Office of the Secretary of Defense
PEO	Program Executive Officer
PPBS	Planning, Programming, and Budgeting System
RCOH	Refueling and complex overhaul
SCN	Shipbuilding and Conversion–Navy

SSBN   Ballistic-missile submarine, nuclear-powered

SSGN   Guided-missile submarine, nuclear-powered

SSN   Submarine, nuclear-powered

Chapter One

INTRODUCTION

The Navy shipbuilding program typically comprises a dozen major projects each year. Many of those projects cost a billion dollars or more each. Furthermore, some of the larger projects occur only once every few years. An aircraft carrier, for example, can cost about $6 billion and, generally, a new start occurs once every four or five years. This combination of a few individually expensive projects and an irregular schedule of new starts can lead to major fluctuations in year-to-year budget totals, even when everything proceeds according to a long-range plan. Unfortunately, major defense acquisition programs rarely exhibit long-term stability: Changing circumstances dictate changing needs; programs run into problems, causing both schedule and cost overruns; etc. Such unplanned fluctuations can exceed a billion dollars in one year, more than can generally be accommodated by intra-year reprogramming actions.

Managing such fluctuating needs for shipbuilding funds is complicated by certain aspects of the budgeting process itself. At the beginning of each Planning, Programming, and Budgeting System (PPBS) cycle, each service is provided fiscal guidance, which represents the total level of resources in all appropriations within which the service is expected to budget all items for its anticipated spending needs. Such guidance triggers a several-step process. First, the Navy generally tries to accommodate its needs for shipbuilding funds, along with other Navy needs, within that fiscal guidance. If adequate funding for shipbuilding cannot be made available in that process, the Navy has the option of using resources from other, presumably lower-priority, Navy programs. Of course, such intra-Navy budget shifting can work the other way. Removing a ship or two from the shipbuilding program often is a pragmatic way for the Navy to solve other funding problems, thus adding to the lack of stability in the shipbuilding account.

In the next step of the triggered process, the Navy forwards its program and budget proposal to the Office of the Secretary of Defense (OSD) for review. OSD has the option of adjusting the proposed shipbuilding budget, possibly moving funds from other defense agencies into or out of the shipbuilding budget. Finally, Congress can make additional adjustments to the proposed shipbuilding budget, either up of down.

The process of managing the shipbuilding budget each year is further complicated by the use of full funding for ships, whereby most of the funding for any U.S. Navy ship is provided in a single year by Congress, even though it may take up to five years to build the ship. This full-funding policy has both advantages and disadvantages relative to other funding alternatives.

An important advantage, and the principal motivation for its institution in the 1950s, is that it lets members of Congress know how much of a commitment they are making to a program when they initially fund it. An important disadvantage is that adjustments to the annual shipbuilding budget must be made in large chunks, each chunk representing the full cost of a ship. This inevitably results in lumpy, irregular year-to-year fluctuations in the total shipbuilding budget, and sometimes limits the most effective use of shipyards and related shipbuilding-industry resources.

In attempts to smooth out the spiky funding profile and provide for greater flexibility in program execution, possible alternatives to full funding have been suggested. For example, ships might be funded incrementally to reflect the amount that must actually be spent that year on construction and nuclear refueling. A second alternative is to create a revolving fund into which a constant amount of money is deposited each year, to be drawn on as needed. A third alternative, known as advance appropriations (AA), involves appropriations of new budget authority that becomes available one or more fiscal years beyond the fiscal year for which the appropriations act was passed, thus spreading out the appropriations for a given project over several years. While not a new appropriation method, AA has not generally been applied to Navy shipbuilding projects (for reasons described in Chapter Two).

Each of these alternatives creates a different set of advantages and disadvantages, which are compared in different ways and from different perspectives in a companion report that focuses on funding for aircraft carriers, the largest single entry in a typical shipbuilding budget (Birkler et al., 2002). In this report, we examine some of the special features of advance appropriations as it might be applied to the Navy shipbuilding program.

STUDY OBJECTIVES

In this study, we considered three issues that arise when contemplating the use of AA for funding ship procurement:

- Exactly what is an advance appropriation, and how might it be applied in different situations and to achieve different objectives?

- How might AA be applied to the Navy Shipbuilding and Conversion (SCN) budget, and what effects might be achieved in SCN budget patterns?

- How are the current and alternative funding profiles likely to affect actions taken by the Navy, the Office of Management and Budget (OMB), OSD, Congress, and shipbuilding contractors in trying to achieve their objectives?

It is important for the reader to understand that much of what we present in these discussions is speculation on how AA might be made to work when applied to Navy shipbuilding projects. To our knowledge, AA has never been applied to military acquisition projects, and there has been very little experience in applying it to non-DoD projects. The government budgeting process is exceedingly complex and dynamic, involving multiple institutions and objectives. Lacking real-world experience on how the competing issues might play out, we limit our discussion to a generalized analysis of the AA process, recognizing that some of our assumptions might prove incorrect and that unforeseen nuances might lead to different results.

OUTLINE OF THE REPORT

Following this Introduction, the remainder of the report is divided into three chapters. Chapter Two presents a summary of how the basic mechanisms of AA can be employed in a project to defer appropriations to later years, how that process can smooth overall appropriation patterns, and how it can create a one-time "perceived surplus" that represents the deferred appropriations. Chapter Three then illustrates, via several examples, how AA could be applied to the SCN budget and what the results could be over time. Chapter Four discusses how the application of AA might be viewed by participants in several offices in the Navy, OSD, OMB, Congress, and industry.

Chapter Two

A BRIEF DESCRIPTION OF ADVANCE APPROPRIATIONS

The procedures involved in advance appropriations and how they can be employed to achieve different objectives are described in this chapter. It is useful to precede the discussion of advance appropriations with a short review of general procedures of government funding and of the full-funding strategy commonly used for funding shipbuilding projects.

FULL FUNDING

The basic process of government funding of weapon acquisition projects involves four steps:

1. The Congress first *authorizes* a particular project to begin in a specified year.

2. The Congress next *appropriates* funds for the project, thus empowering the contracting agent to obligate the expenditure of government funds for the specified project.

3. An appropriate contracting agent *obligates* expenditure of the funds, typically through a contract with a commercial firm.

4. The funds are then *disbursed* to the firm according to the terms of the contract.

In a typical fully funded project, each of the first two steps occurs once; the project is authorized, and funds sufficient to complete the project are appropriated. The subsequent contracting and dis-

the fiscal year for which the appropriation act was passed" (Section 20, p. 24). "Advance Appropriations are enacted normally in the current year, scored after the budget year, and available for obligation in the year scored and subsequent years if specified in the language" (Appendix 300A, p. 569).

- "Capital projects or useful segments of capital projects must be *fully funded* either through regular or advance appropriations. *Full funding* means that appropriations—regular annual appropriations or advance appropriations—are enacted that are sufficient in total to complete a useful segment of a capital project before any obligations may be incurred for that segment . . . . Full funding for an entire capital project is required if the project cannot be divided into more than one useful segment" (Section 300, p. 549).

- "Regular appropriations for the full funding of a capital project or a useful segment of a capital project in the budget year are preferred. If this results in spikes that, in the judgment of OMB, cannot be accommodated by the agency or the Congress, a combination of regular and advance appropriations that together provide full funding for a capital project or a useful segment should be proposed in the budget" (Appendix 300A, p. 566).

  That section goes on to say in a later paragraph that "Advance appropriations have the same benefit as regular appropriations for improving planning, management and the accountability of the project."

Full funding is the preferred appropriation method. However, there is an allowance for the use of advance appropriations, which is like full funding in that the full cost of the project is stated up front. Unlike full funding, advance appropriations commits funds from future-year budgets, thus denying use of those funds to the Congresses in those future years.

ALTERNATIVE WAYS OF USING ADVANCE APPROPRIATIONS

Compared with the traditional practice of fully funding each new project in a single year, use of advance appropriations results in decreasing the budget in the initial year of the project and increasing the budget in one or more of the following years. This basic strategy can be applied to achieve any of three different objectives:

1. By spreading the funding of any acquisition over several years, AA can smooth out peaks and valleys in the overall budget.

2. If applying AA to a particular project does not affect the total shipbuilding budget, that application releases budgetary funds that can be applied elsewhere in the first year. That "additional" budget must then be repaid in the future years covered by the AA action. The effect is that of borrowing against the near future.

3. Again assuming an unchanged total shipbuilding budget level, repeated application of AA across several projects can push the date of repayment so far into the future that repayment is irrelevant to the current planning and execution of the budget, thus creating a "perceived surplus" that can be applied elsewhere.

Some additional aspects of advance appropriations, including its possible effects on use of multiyear procurement and how its use might be perceived from different institutional perspectives, are discussed in Chapter Four. In the remainder of this chapter, we describe each of the three applications of AA and illustrate how the underlying mechanisms work.[3]

SMOOTHING THE BUDGET PATTERN

An occasional purchase of an exceptionally costly item can cause sharp discontinuities in the overall shipbuilding budget patterns. For example, an aircraft carrier, if funded entirely in one year, can cause a jump of 20 to 30 percent in the overall shipbuilding budget. However, construction of a carrier typically extends over a period of

---

[3]It is important to note that in the second and third applications noted above, we assume that the total shipbuilding budget remains unchanged, so that application of AA to one or more projects creates some new increment of funds in the initial year of the projects, and that the money thus freed up can be applied to some other project by the Navy. Whether it is realistic to expect Congress to take a hands-off approach in such a situation remains to be seen. We make this assumption only to illustrate one theoretical consequence of applying AA to a procurement project.

about five years, so an appropriation for the entire cost does not have to be available in the first year. Past experience suggests that contractor costs could be covered by appropriating, and funding, 35 percent of the total cost in each of the first two years, 20 percent in the third year, and 10 percent in the fourth year (i.e., a *funding profile* of 35–35–20–10 percent). A new aircraft carrier is usually started about every five years, which means that the entire cost of a ship funded in this manner would be paid before the start of the next ship, and the overall shipbuilding budget would show less year-to-year fluctuation.

Figure 2.1 illustrates, for comparison, the traditional full-funding strategy and an advance-appropriations strategy. Suppose that an average shipbuilding budget is $15 billion per year for all ships except aircraft carriers. The full funding of a new carrier once every five years at a unit cost of $6 billion would result in the pattern for the total shipbuilding budget shown in Figure 2.1a. If the appropriations were spread over a period of four years, in the funding profile suggested above, the resulting total shipbuilding budget pattern would be that in Figure 2.1b.

This simplified illustration assumes that the remainder of the ship construction budget will stay constant throughout the period shown—a situation that rarely occurs. The true effect of applying AA to a particular budget element will depend on how that project meshes with the peaks and valleys of the overall budget that are caused by the schedules of other projects. The complex interaction of AA-funded projects and fully funded projects in a real-world situation is illustrated in Chapter Three.

This application of AA corresponds to that envisioned in OMB *Circular A-11*. Although the application of AA to one or more shipbuilding programs might not yield a completely smooth total budget pattern, it clearly provides a tool that the budget manager might find useful when trying to minimize budget perturbations. However, we do not have experience on which to judge whether that theoretical advantage can be realized in practice.

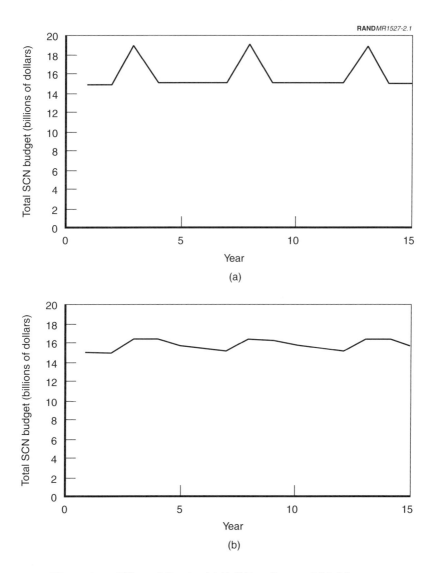

**Figure 2.1—Effect of Carrier (a) Full Funding and (b) Advance
Appropriations on the SCN Budget**

CREATING A SHORT-TERM LOAN AGAINST THE FUTURE

The use of AA can create the equivalent of a short-term loan, to be paid back in the near future. Consider an example in which the Navy proposes a FY2002–FY2006 shipbuilding budget that includes a nuclear submarine to be started in 2002, at a cost of $2 billion, and a special-purpose ship to be started in 2003, at a cost of $1 billion. Each ship is to be fully funded in the year of construction start.

Now suppose that, in mid-2001, a situation arose making it desirable to move the start of the special-purpose ship ahead one year, to 2002. But also suppose that other circumstances made it very difficult to increase the 2002 budget by the extra $1 billion needed for such a move. That situation might be handled by changing the submarine appropriation to an advance appropriation, calling for $1 billion to be appropriated in 2002 and the remaining $1 billion to be appropriated in 2003. Such a procedure would cover the appropriations and expenditures needed for the submarine project *and* would make available $1 billion in 2002 to start the special-purpose ship without any change in the total shipbuilding budget level.

This example represents a zero-sum transfer and, while not the sort of application discussed in OMB *Circular A-11*, seems like an application that might be found acceptable by OMB and Congress. The "loan" from the submarine program in 2002 would be "repaid" in 2003 from the money that had been originally scheduled for the special-purpose ship in that year. It seems plausible that AA could be useful in resolving budget problems of the type postulated here.

We can envision another kind of short-term loan that could be created through use of AA. Suppose that, in the above example, no special-purpose ship had been presented in the budget items for start in 2003, but that an urgent need arose some time in 2001 to start such a ship in 2002. The same shift from full funding to AA for the submarine could again free up the needed $1 billion in FY2002 funds, but that money would have to be repaid to the submarine program in FY2003. Perhaps Congress would increase the FY2003 budget by the needed $1 billion or shift the funds from some other account.

This use of AA to fund a new program no longer represents a zero-sum transfer of funds between programs and budget years. Instead, it becomes a loan against the future without a specified repayment plan.

In these examples, and in the following discussion of a long-term loan against the future, we assume that the original total budget level remains unchanged when AA is applied to one or more projects, thus reducing the funds needed for those projects in the first year and freeing up the reduced amount to be applied to other uses. Of course, there is no guarantee that Congress will leave those "freed-up" funds in the original budget category or approve their use for some other purpose within that budget category. However, such an assumption is necessary for the "loan" concept to work. We make that assumption for the purposes of illustrating the effect.

CREATING A LONG-TERM LOAN AGAINST THE FUTURE

Under some circumstances, advance appropriations could create near-term funds that would not require payback until some time in the indefinite future. This use of AA appears far outside the model envisioned in OMB *Circular A-11*, and there is no guarantee that any Congress would agree to such use. However, the strategy has obvious appeal to budget managers and has been advocated by some officials in the DoD. For these reasons, we illustrate the basic mechanism here. In Chapter Three, we show how that mechanism might be applied to Navy shipbuilding budgets.

In the illustration directly above, the Navy would obtain $1 billion that had not previously been presented in the budget items for 2002, but it would have to pay that money back to the submarine project in 2003. Now, suppose that the payback was achieved by opening a new AA account in 2003 for the submarine scheduled to be started that year. That would free up the needed $1 billion in FY2003 funds, effectively borrowing it against the FY2004 budget.

Suppose further that this tactic is repeated in FY2004 and in every successive year. The payback can be deferred as long as the submarine program is scheduled to start a new boat every year. Thus, the near-term appearance is that of "finding" a new $1 billion in FY2002. Of course, that result is predicated on the Navy successfully funding a new submarine start every year, thus enabling the loan to be rolled over year after year. We illustrate this process using a simple, one-product model.

A Simple Model to Illustrate Use of AA to Create a Long-Term Loan

To develop a model of AA for creating a long-term loan, we consider a program in which one new copy of an item (*j*) is ordered every year (*i*) at a cost of $100.[4] We further assume that assembly of the product is lengthy and that final delivery is several years after the order date. Under a full-funding strategy, the purchasing agency would budget, and obligate, the full purchase price of $100 every year. We further assume that, after using a full-funding strategy for the first two annual buys, the purchasing agency shifts to AA , using a 40–30–20–10 percent funding profile. That is, only 40 percent of the full cost is appropriated in the year of purchase, 30 percent is appropriated in the second year, 20 percent in the third year, and 10 percent in the fourth year. The results are shown in Table 2.1, where we first show two years of traditional full funding to establish a reference point, then apply the AA funding profile for each purchase in years 3 through 7, with no purchase in subsequent years. The full history of appropriations (expenditures) for each item purchased is displayed in a separate row.

The three rows of entries at the bottom of the table need to be differentiated to make AA comprehensible. The first, labeled "Total annual appropriation," represents the sum of all expenditures in any particular year and, hence, the sum of all appropriations required in any single year to support the series of procurements postulated in the example. In any such program involving repeated procurement of the same item year after year, it can readily be seen that, *after the initial transition period, the annual expenditure (and appropriation) required is the same as the total cost of each annual buy.* The total appropriation needed during the steady-state period is the same for AA as it is for full funding. It is only during the transition periods, at the beginning and end of the program, that the annual appropriation

---

[4]The assumption of repetitive annual procurement is critical to this example. A sporadic procurement program leads to different results, as discussed in Chapter Three.

Table 2.1

Illustration of Accumulated Deferred Appropriations

Year (i)	1	2	3	4	5	6	7	8	9	10	11
Number of items procured (j)	1	1	1	1	1	1	1	0	0	0	0
Funding profile for first buy	$100										
Funding profile for second buy		$100									
Funding profile for third buy			$40	$30	$20	$10					
Funding profile for fourth buy				$40	$30	$20	$10				
Funding profile for fifth buy					$40	$30	$20	$10			
Funding profile for sixth buy						$40	$30	$20	$10		
Funding profile for seventh (last) buy							$40	$30	$20	$10	
Total annual appropriation	$100	$100	$40	$70	$90	$100	$100	$60	$30	$10	$0
Annual increment of new deferred appropriation			$60	$30	$10	$0	$0	$0			
Accumulated deferred appropriation			$60	$90	$100	$100	$100	$60	$30	$10	$0

needed under AA is different from that needed for the same program under full funding.

The second row at the bottom of Table 2.1 shows the new increment of appropriation that is deferred *each year*. This deferred value is the difference between the cost of each annual buy ($100 in this example) and the expenditure (appropriation) required in each individual year.

The third row shows the accumulation of those annual increments of deferred appropriation, representing funds that could have been appropriated for some other activity, *assuming no change in the total budget*. Of course, that "surplus" will have to be repaid at some time in the future after the program ends. This third row also shows how the accumulation is "paid back" during the several years at the end of

the program after new procurement has ended. If the annual procurement had continued far into the future, the "payback" of the accumulated surplus would be deferred similarly.

The effect of applying AA to one program, as illustrated in Table 2.1,
is exactly the same as an individual or firm using a line of credit: One
year's borrowing is paid back in the following year, but an equal
amount of new funds is borrowed in that following year. Thus, as
long as the process is continued, the initial amount borrowed in the
first year remains in the pocket of the borrower, with each year of
payback balanced by new borrowing. Nevertheless, that initial
amount borrowed remains as a debt and must eventually be paid
back to the lender. Of course, the appropriations process as performed by Congress functions differently than a commercial
borrower-lender relationship. In a procurement program extending
over several years, it is unlikely that Congress would insist on debit-
ing some future-year appropriations to "pay back" a perceived surplus created at the beginning of the program.

We can now derive a generalized method for determining the AA-
generated accumulated "deferred appropriation" available at any
point, compared with a continuation of full funding.

Let

$X_{i,j}$ = percent of total procurement cost appropriated in year i for
item j, where item j is one of a series of similar items procured in an
ongoing program, so that

$$X_{i=1} + X_{i=2} + X_{i=3} + \ldots + X_{i=N}$$
$$= 100 \text{ percent for each item } j \text{ procured.} \qquad (2.1)$$

For the class of items $j_1, j_2, j_3, \ldots, j_N$, the total amount of deferred
appropriation (DA) that will exist in any year can be expressed as

$$DA_j = X_2 + 2X_3 + 3X_4 + \ldots + (N-1)X_N \qquad (2.2)$$

The validity of this expression can be verified by observing the data
in Table 2.2, which reproduces portions of Table 2.1. At the end of
year 5, for example, the deferred appropriations shown in the shaded
area equal $30 (the first year of deferred appropriations from the fifth

Table 2.2

Determination of Accumulated Deferred Appropriations

Year	1	2	3	4	5	6	7	8	9	10	11
Number of items procured	1	1	1	1	1	1	1	0	0	0	0
Funding profile for first buy	$100										
Funding profile for second buy		$100									
Funding profile for third buy				$40	$30	$20	$10				
Funding profile for fourth buy					$40	$30	$20	$10			
Funding profile for fifth buy						$40	$30	$20	$10		

NOTE: Shading indicates everything that includes a future appropriation in year 5.

buy), plus (2 × $20) (the second-year deferred appropriations from the fourth and fifth buys) plus (3 × $10) (the third-year deferred appropriations from the third, fourth, and fifth buys).

The amount of appropriations that can be deferred in any particular procurement program depends on the schedule for which obligations, and therefore appropriations, are needed for that particular project.[5] Examples of the accumulated deferred appropriations are shown in Table 2.3. Given a funding profile of 40–20–20–20 percent, we see that a one-time "perceived budget surplus" equal to 120 percent of the steady-state annual budget for that program will be accumulated under the advance-appropriations process over the first four years.

The total amount of deferred appropriation for an entire budget category (such as shipbuilding) can be determined by summing the deferred appropriations across all programs currently being funded under advance appropriations. *If the total appropriation for the entire budget category remains relatively constant over a period of years,*

---

[5]The necessary schedule of appropriations and expenditures over time will depend on the characteristics of each project. The various schedules shown in these examples are created notionally to illustrate the process, and none is necessarily practical for a specific project.

Table 2.3

Effect of Funding Profile on Amount of Accumulated Deferred Appropriation

Funding Profile (annual percent of item procurement cost)	Steady-State Accumulated Deferred Appropriation (percent of item procurement cost)
60–40	40
50–50	50
60–30–10	50
50–30–20	70
50–25–25	75
40–30–20–10	100
35–35–20–10	105
40–20–20–20	120
30–30–30–10	120
30–30–20–20	130

then the application of AA to all programs under that budget category could yield a one-time, accumulated deferred appropriation totaling a major fraction of the total annual budget. How that "surplus" might be used is, of course, subject to the proposals of the administration and to subsequent congressional action, but it would create a substantial sum of money that would represent long-term borrowing against the future and that could be used for other near-term applications.

CONSTRAINTS ON MANAGEMENT'S ABILITY TO MODIFY THE SHIPBUILDING PROGRAM

The application of AA to the Navy shipbuilding program can have both positive and negative effects on senior management's ability to modify the program in response to changing environments.

Program Initiation and Termination

If a shipbuilding program being funded under AA were terminated (and we admit that this is *not* a likely occurrence), the effect would be roughly the same as that under full funding: Appropriate liabilities would have to be paid on open contracts, and money appropriated but not obligated would become available for other uses. Conversely, the start of a new shipbuilding program funded under AA would not require full appropriation the first year; instead, the budget consequences would build up over a period of several years. If one program funded by AA were terminated and replaced with another program of approximately the same cost and funding profile, the effects on the total budget each year would be negligible as the tail-off in spending (and in corresponding appropriations) for the terminated program meshed with the buildup in appropriations on the new program. None of these effects should pose significant problems to budget management, provided that events evolve in a way generally consistent with expectations incorporated in the future-year program. Furthermore, events that lead to an increase in available budget should create no exceptional problems to budget management under AA.

Coping with a Budget Cut

If there is a reduction in overall shipbuilding budget and that reduction has not been incorporated in prior presentation of budget items, widespread application of AA to the Navy shipbuilding program could lead to special challenges. To illustrate this effect, let us assume that AA is applied to the entire shipbuilding program over the next few years. In any typical year thereafter, over half of the annual budget would be devoted to paying the future-year deferred appropriation of prior-year buys. Taking into account that some of the budget is devoted to advance procurement, it is likely that as little as 40 percent of a typical year's budget would be available to fund new shipbuilding starts in any year. Now assume that an unexpected cut of 10 percent is imposed on the overall budget in some future year. Taking that entire cut out of the 40 percent available for new starts would lead to a 25-percent reduction in new starts that could be funded that year (see Table 3.5 and related discussion).

SUMMARY OBSERVATIONS

This broad overview of the AA strategy leads to three general observations about the effects to be expected from applying the strategy to Navy shipbuilding:

- Application to special, very large projects such as aircraft carriers could reduce the magnitude of total-budget spikes created by such projects.

- Widespread application of advance appropriations to a substantial fraction of the total shipbuilding program would yield a one-time perceived surplus that could be applied to near-term, one-time expenditures, pending approval of Congress.

- Widespread application could complicate the ability of senior management to accommodate unexpected downward changes in the shipbuilding budget in future years.

Chapter Three

APPLICATION OF ADVANCE APPROPRIATIONS TO THE SCN BUDGET

In the preceding chapter, we described some of the basic applications of AA and explored how those applications can affect budget management. In this chapter, we illustrate how AA might be applied to the SCN budget over the next two decades. Without attempting to recommend any application, we have as our objective to inform the reader on possible applications of AA.

In Chapter Two, we considered three possible objectives for the use of AA. In this chapter, we illustrate only two of those: the effect of reducing short-term spikes in the total budget, and the creation of a long-term loan against the future (a perceived near-term surplus). The application of AA to create a short-term loan for improving management of a specific budgeting problem seems sufficiently intuitive, and admits to so many possible variations, that illustration seemed both unreasonably complex and unnecessary.

ANALYSIS METHODS AND DATA

This analysis was performed using a spreadsheet accounting model developed specifically for it. Such a model enables overall SCN budget consequences to be tracked after certain assumptions have been made about the application of AA to one or more elements of the ship-acquisition program. Here, we discuss the data that were input into the analysis.

The planned fleet composition was adopted from the *Report on Naval Vessel Force Structure Requirements* (Cohen, 2000), as submitted to the Senate Armed Services Committee on June 26, 2000. That report contains a table entitled "Long-Range Plan 2001–2030," repeated here as Table 3.1 (years 2026–2030 omitted), showing the year-to-year procurements of major ships as planned by the Navy in 2000. Any plan such as this will change from time to time, and the data in Table 3.1 are undoubtedly different from those of the most recent plan. However, assuming that the broad structure and overall size of the postulated Fleet have not changed, the data shown will suffice to illustrate the important aspects of AA application.

The costs used in the analysis are shown in Table 3.2. As for the procurement schedule shown in Table 3.1, these costs are certainly not exactly those that will be incurred, but they are close enough to serve the needs of the present analysis.

The final set of input data needed to perform this analysis is the funding profile and, hence, the required appropriation schedule, assumed for each ship to which AA is applied. The profiles used in the present analysis are shown in Table 3.3. All advance-procurement funds are assumed to be obligated in the year appropriated.

The assumptions on funding profile can have a considerable effect on the subsequent analysis results. As shown in Chapter Two, deferring a substantial fraction of the appropriations to later years has a strong effect on the size of the one-time surplus created.

BASE CASE

Using the procurement schedule and assumed costs shown in Tables 3.1 and 3.2, we can construct a reference case that represents the expected overall Navy ship-procurement program and required budget over the next 25 years, assuming traditional full funding of each ship in the year the construction starts. A curve representing the resulting overall SCN budget is shown in Figure 3.1. Note that, to maintain a constant fleet size of about 300 ships, it will be necessary for the budget to rise from about $7 billion in 2002 to about $17 billion in 2025. This increase is an important component in some of the results shown below, especially those dealing with the creation of a one-time budget surplus.

Table 3.1
Long-Range Plan of Shipbuilding, by Type per Year, 2001 through 2025

Ship Type	Year																								
	01	02	03	04	05	06	07	08	09	10	11	12	13	14	15	16	17	18	19	20	21	22	23	24	25
CVN	1					1					1					1				1				1	
SSN/SSBN	1	1	1	1	1	1	2	2	3	3	2	3	3	3	3	2	3	3	2	3	3	3	2	3	3
DDG-51/DD-21	3	2	2	2	2	2	3	3	3	3	3	3	3	4	3	4	5	3	3	3	3	4	4	4	4
LPD/LHD	2	2	2	2	1																				
Amphibious								1				1			1			1		1	1	2	1	1	2
JCC				1	1	1	1																		
T-AKE	1	3	3	2	2																				
Logistics																			1	2	2	2	2	2	2
Support										1	1	1	4	3	3	5	4	4	2	1	1	1	1	1	1
Total Procured	8	8	8	8	7	5	6	6	6	7	7	8	10	10	10	12	12	11	8	11	10	12	10	12	12
Total Fleet size	316	315	313	313	313	311	311	304	305	305	305	305	309	305	305	304	300	301	305	309	308	310	301	303	302

Table 3.2

Assumed Values of Ship-Procurement Costs

Description	Year	Total Obligation Authority ($M 2000)	Advance Procure- ment ($M 2000)
CVNX1	2006	4,159	2,156
CVNX2	2011	4,227	1,710
CVNX3	2016	3,780	1408
CVNX4	2020	3,780	1,408
CVNX5	2024	3,780	1,408
CVNX6	2028	3,780	1,408
RCOH CVN 70	2005	2,002	687
RCOH CVN 71	2009	2,002	687
RCOH CVN 72	2012	2,002	687
RCOH CVN 73	2015	2,002	687
RCOH CVN 74	2018	2,002	687
RCOH CVN 75	2021	2,002	687
RCOH CVN 76	2025	2,002	687
RCOH CVN 77	2031	2,002	687
SSN	2001	1,500	500
SSBN	2020	2,000	750
DDG-51	2005	800	75
DD-21	2005	1,200	100
LPD-17	2001	600	100
LHD-8	2005	1,200	200
LPD (X)	2008	750	50
JCC (X)	2004	350	100
AKE (X)	2001	300	100
Auxiliary	2019	350	100
LSD	2010	300	100

EFFECTS OF APPLYING AA TO THE SCN PROGRAM

We examine three scenarios for applying AA to the funding of various elements of the overall SCN program:

- Apply AA only to construction of CVNs.

- Apply AA to procurement of all ships in a class (we use Surface Combatants [DDG and DD] in our example).

- Apply AA to the entire Navy ship-procurement program.

Table 3.3

**Assumed Profiles of Advance-Appropriations Funding
(percentage of TOA from Table 3.2)**

Ship Class	Year 1 (%)	Year 2 (%)	Year 3 (%)	Year 4 (%)
CVN	35	35	20	10
SSN/SSBN	50	35	15	
DDG-51/ DD-21	50	30	20	
LPD	60	30	10	
LHD	50	25	25	
LHD(X)	50	25	25	
JCC(X)	60	30	10	
AKE(X)	60	40		
Auxiliary	60	40		
LSD	60	40		

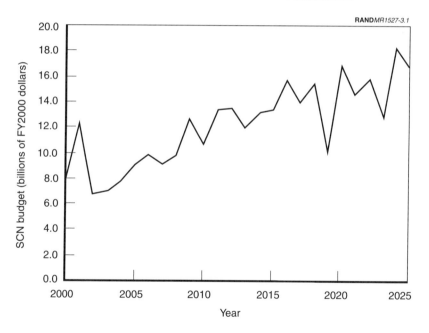

Figure 3.1—Projected SCN Budget, Full Funding

For all cases, AA will be applied to the FY2003 and subsequent budgets. For each case, we display the two consequences of AA that are directly quantitative:

- The smoothing of peaks and valleys in the overall budget caused by spreading the appropriations of any acquisition over several years.

- The one-time "surplus" created through deferring part of the appropriations to future years.

Finally, we illustrate how extensive application of AA could constrain the flexibility of management to change fleet composition and overall budget levels. In each of the following illustrations, we assume that when AA is applied to one or more ship-procurement programs, no changes are made in any of the other programs in the overall SCN budget for the years examined. This is not necessarily a realistic assumption, but it is a useful way of illustrating the basic consequences of using AA.

Use of AA in Funding of Aircraft Carrier New Construction

Aircraft carriers represent large single-transaction costs. Here, we assume that AA is used to budget carrier procurement, starting with the FY2003 budget.

Total-Budget Smoothing.   The use of AA for funding occasional, large projects such as an aircraft carrier is expected to result in smaller perturbations in the overall SCN budget than would result with full funding. As shown in Figure 3.2, the use of AA to fund procurement and major overhaul of aircraft carriers can lead to overall budget changes of over $2 billion in any individual year when compared with conventional full funding of those same activities. However, whether those changes lead to significant smoothing of the total budget depends on how the AA-funded projects mesh with other projects in each particular year.

Assuming all other shipbuilding projects are fully funded, the total SCN budget for those projects will inevitably fluctuate from year to year, and the application of AA to one particular element (such as aircraft carrier construction) could result in an increase or decrease

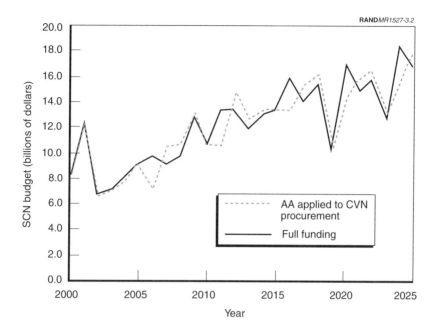

Figure 3.2—Change in SCN Budget Variability After AA Is Applied to
Aircraft Carrier New Construction

in the total SCN budget, depending on how the projects mesh over
time. Thus, use of AA for a particular component of the ship-
procurement program does not automatically lead to smoother total
SCN budgets. Whether use of AA would be useful to Navy budget
managers seems to depend on circumstances that prevail in a particular year.

Creation of a Perceived Surplus. The "perceived surplus" created by
applying AA is plotted in Figure 3.3. The large cost of the carrier,
combined with the spreading of a major portion of the cost over several future years, leads to maximum values of about $2.5 billion be-
ing deferred at certain points in time (2005, 2010, and 2015 in the figure). However, those deferred appropriations are amortized over
three years, whereas the next carrier is not started for about five
years. Therefore, no long-term fund is created that could be used for
other purposes without almost immediate payback of the funds.

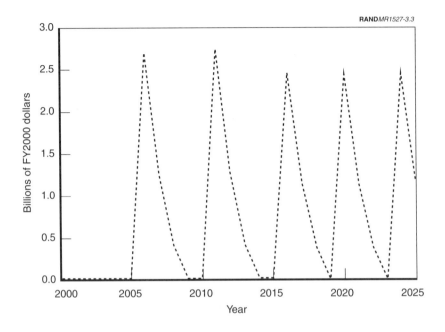

Figure 3.3—"Perceived Surplus" Created When AA Is Applied
to CVN New-Construction Budget

This situation is equivalent to the short-term loan application described in Chapter Two.

Use of AA in Funding of All Surface Combatants (DDG-51 and DD-21 Classes)

Total-SCN-Budget Smoothing. The Navy plans to procure several new destroyer ships each year. The profile of deferred appropriations for destroyers extends only two years into the future. Therefore, applying AA to the budget for construction of new destroyers yields only modest smoothing of the overall SCN budget line, as shown in Figure 3.4. The net results on the overall SCN budget patterns are relatively small.

Creation of a Perceived Surplus. The Surface Combatant program is essentially continuous. Application of AA to such a program leads to a substantial element of the budget being deferred until the end of

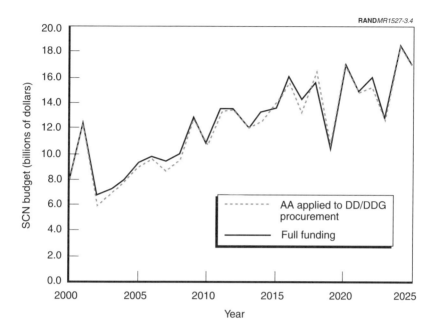

**Figure 3.4—Change in SCN Budget Variability When AA Is Applied to
DDG-51 and DD-21 Procurements**

the program, which is in the distant future. The one-time surplus
created by applying AA to the DDG-51 and DD-21 budgets is shown
in Figure 3.5. It is different from the case of the aircraft carrier funding discussed above.

This surplus effect can be illustrated by examining the year 2010.
The funding profile for the DDG/DD classes is 50–30–20 percent. In
the years 2008 through 2012, the Navy plans to procure three ships
each year, for an annual cost of $3.6 billion, yielding the appropria-
tion schedule for 2009 and 2010 shown in Table 3.4. The third-year
deferred appropriation for the 2009 buy is $720 million (20 percent of
the total 2009 buy of $3.6 billion), plus the second- and third-year
deferred appropriation for the 2010 buy of $1.080 billion (30 percent
of the total 2010 buy of $3.6 billion) and $720 million (20 percent of
the total 2010 buy of $3.6 billion), which yields a total accumulated
surplus of $2.520 billion.

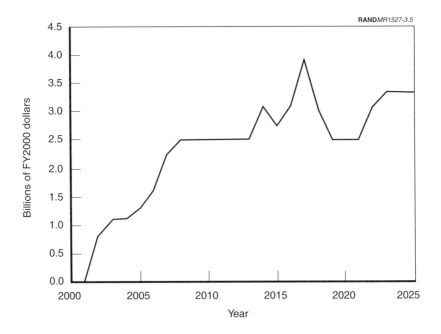

Figure 3.5—"Accumulated Surplus" Created When AA Is Applied to DDG-51 and DD-21 Budgets

Table 3.4

Distribution of Budget-Year and Deferred Appropriations for Procurement of Three Destroyers in Each of Two Successive Years

	Billions of 2000 Dollars			
Year	2009	2010	2011	2012
2009 buy	$1.800	$1.080	$0 .720	
2010 buy		$1.800	$1.080	$0.720
Accumulated perceived surplus in 2010			$1.800	$0.720

NOTE: Shading indicates accumulated surplus.

As long as the Navy continues to buy three destroyers each year, that accumulated surplus will remain constant. The actual plan used in the analysis calls for the procurement rate to fluctuate between three

and five per year in the succeeding years, thus leading to the fluctuation in accumulated surplus shown in Figure 3.5.

It is apparent that the accumulated surplus in a long-term program
involving repetitive procurement of many ships is fundamentally different from that of an aircraft carrier, for which the accumulated
surplus is liquidated before the start of the next carrier. In a long-
term program such as that illustrated here, the "payback" period is
deferred into the indefinite future. In principle, the payback period
could be deferred indefinitely by rolling over the loan by applying AA
to other new ships at the end of the destroyer production run.

Use of AA in Funding of All Ship Procurement

Total-SCN-Budget Smoothing. Use of AA for all ship procurement
has a substantial smoothing effect on the overall budget pattern, as
shown in Figure 3.6.

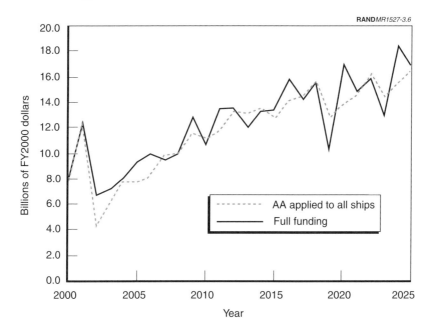

Figure 3.6—Effect of Applying AA to All Navy Ship Procurement

Creation of a Perceived Surplus. If the AA strategy is applied to all ship procurement starting in FY2003, a "perceived surplus" with a value in excess of $6 billion after about 2010 is created, as shown in Figure 3.7, as the overall procurement program approaches a size greater than $14 billion annually. As long as the budget does not experience a significant cut, that "loan against the future" is sustained and available for other uses, subject to the agreement of Congress. In the real world, budgets are always subject to great pressure and any perceived surplus such as that created by broad application of AA to ship-procurement projects would be targeted for many possible applications in addition to other ship procurements.

Such shifting of "surplus" funds to other applications outside the shipbuilding budget would clearly make the AA concept less attractive, especially to those managing the Navy shipbuilding program.

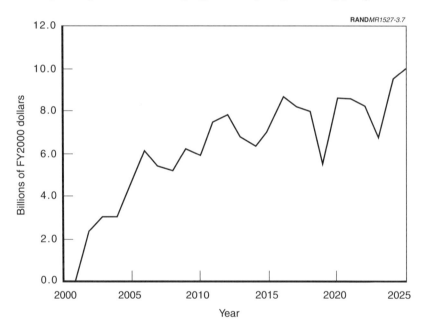

Figure 3.7—Accumulated "Perceived Surplus" Created When AA Is
Applied to All Navy Ship Procurement

WIDESPREAD APPLICATION OF AA TO THE NAVY SHIPBUILDING PROGRAM HAS POTENTIAL DISADVANTAGES

The illustrations discussed above tend to show results of applying AA that could be viewed as positive by some managers under certain circumstances. However, the apparent benefits are not without some corresponding disadvantages and risks.

One of the risks of widespread application of AA is that, if the budget is decreased for some reason, only part of the budget is directly available to absorb the cut. For example, consider budget year 2010 in the case for which AA is applied to all ship procurement. The full complement of SCN budget elements for that year is shown in Table 3.5. We include the advance-procurement elements in the table because, while not affected directly by AA, they represent an obligation to ongoing programs.   In that year, only 39 percent of the total budget is assigned to new-project starts; the remainder is assigned to deferred expenditures for programs started in prior years or to AP for programs that have been started but that have not yet reached the construction-start year.

Table 3.5

Projected Distribution of Major Cost Elements in the SCN Budget in FY2010 If AA Is Applied to All Programs

Ship	New Construction ($M FY2000)	Deferred Portion of Prior-Year Appropriations ($M FY2000)	Advance Procurement ($M FY2000)
CVNX2			89
CVN 71 RCOH		600	
CVN 72 RCOH			270
SSN	2,250	2,025	1,500
DD-21	1,800	1,800	300
LPD		75	
Auxiliary	180		100
Total	4,230	4,500	2,170
Portion of total FY2010 SCN budget	39%	41%	20%
Total after 10% budget cut	3,140	4,500	2,170

Now, assume that the available budget for shipbuilding in 2010 is cut by 10 percent from prior-year plans (not an exceptional occurrence). If we wish to avoid the costs associated with stretching the funding of ongoing programs over longer periods, then the cut of $1.09 billion would be taken entirely from the $4.23 billion available for new starts, reducing that amount to $3.14 billion, roughly a 25-percent reduction. Since much of the funding for any one year is committed to projects already started, the widespread application of AA tends to amplify any reductions in the budget.

Chapter Four

OTHER CONSIDERATIONS

In the first three chapters of this report, we have described how advance appropriations might be applied to the shipbuilding budget and the likely consequences of such a budgetary strategy. In this chapter, we briefly examine two other aspects of applying AA to the Navy shipbuilding budget: opportunities for cost reductions and some possible implementation issues. We have not examined these aspects quantitatively or in detail; we offer them as initial explorations of complex matters.

USING ADVANCE APPROPRIATIONS TO REALIZE COST-REDUCTION OPPORTUNITIES

The application of AA appears to have no *direct* effect on the cost of building a ship. Spreading out the appropriation neither creates nor destroys money. A $6-billion aircraft carrier still costs $6 billion. However, use of AA might turn out to be an enabling factor in other strategies that do have some cost-reduction capabilities, particularly multiyear procurement (MYP).

In MYP, the Navy contracts with a shipyard to build multiple ships over a specified period of time. The advantage to the shipyard is that it can balance its workload and manpower fluctuations and order material in the most cost-effective manner. Some shipbuilders have indicated that MYP (combined with appropriate termination liability) would enable them to build ships in segments—for example, constructing the ship bridge for several ships at a time—and store the segments until needed, thus reducing costs. Limited experience with MYP in procurement of various kinds of weapon systems suggests that savings of 3 to 10 percent can be achieved over conventional single-year procurements.

Despite these claimed advantages, the Navy has not made wide use of MYP in shipbuilding. The Navy and DoD oppose MYP mainly because it reduces future management flexibility. Future shipbuilding funds cannot be shifted to other uses without canceling the MYP contract and incurring the additional costs that such cancellation entails. However, AA already commits appropriations in future years. Therefore, it might be appropriate to expand a single-year procurement using AA to a multiyear procurement and realize the cost reduction that doing so would provide.

IMPLEMENTING ADVANCE APPROPRIATIONS: SOME ISSUES

The shipbuilding process and industry go back to the founding days of the Republic, and new ideas must pass a rigorous test in the marketplace. The use of AA to fund shipbuilding would be a new and untried practice and is viewed by many as undesirable. It is worthwhile to briefly examine these various viewpoints.

Viewpoints on the viability of AA depend upon "where you sit."[1] We have compared the present funding strategy with the suggested AA strategy from a series of differing perspectives:[2]

- Contractor
- Program Executive Officers in the Navy
- Navy leadership
- Office of the Secretary of Defense
- Office of Management and Budget
- Congress.

---

[1]This information is a result of general discussions with various Navy, DoD, industry, and congressional leaders, as well as articles that have appeared in various print media over the past year, 2001. Meant to illustrate the breadth of viewpoints on the issue of the use of advance appropriations, it is not prescriptive.

[2]Throughout this examination, we have retained our earlier assumption that AA will not change the Navy's overall budget.

Each of these organizations has a different bias and logic for either positive or negative positions on the AA proposal. These different perspectives are outlined below.

Contractor

First, let's examine the contractor's perspective. A summary is shown in Table 4.1.

On the positive side, the contractors have stated that the single reason they prefer AA is that it would limit the government's opportunity to change procurement plans, particularly in programs that have multiple ship buys over the Future Years Defense Plan. Once the Navy has embarked on a plan to advance appropriate funds for a given type of ship, it would be difficult to request appropriations for the next year's ship of the class with full funding. And, given the stream of dollars in the future years, it would also be more difficult for the Navy to truncate a procurement once that procurement was started. The contractors believe that that constraint would limit the Navy and prevent movement of dollars from the SCN budget to other budgets, thus encouraging long-range planning by shipbuilders.

At the same time, given that the Navy had locked up its future-year budgets in AA, MYP would become more viable. The foremost reason programmers and budgeters in the Navy have given for opposing MYP is that it would force the Navy to buy the commodity in the future years and thus reduce the flexibility of the leadership to change its priorities. Given that AA already reduces leadership flexibility, MYP becomes a natural consequence of AA. Finally, AA does not preclude the need for termination-liability funding on the

Table 4.1

Contractor Perspective on AA

Pros	Cons
Stabilizes the near-term and long-term budgets	Must go to Congress with any fiscal changes in the future years
Encourages long-range planning by shipbuilders	Not as simple as conventional full funding
Makes MYP more attractive	
Has termination liability as a cost	

part of the government, so the contractor still has protection from termination.

A "con" for the shipbuilder is that the simplicity of single-year full funding would be lost. Any changes must go to Congress. Finally, a con for the shipbuilder is that, because a ship procurement under AA would involve making outlays over three to eight years (depending upon the ship), it is less likely that Congress would add a ship in the future years.

Program Executive Officer

Our second perspective is that of the Program Executive Officer (PEO), the admiral who manages a series of ship-procurement programs that would individually or collectively be affected by the AA process. Table 4.2 describes the pros and cons of this perspective.

The PEO looks at his program from a unique perspective. His goal is to deliver a ship to the Navy on time and within cost constraints, with as little oversight as possible. From the positive viewpoint, AA, like full funding in a single year, would provide stability. In fact, AA may be even more stable: Once the Navy starts down that road for the entire shipbuilding appropriation, it is less likely that it would remove ships from the approved future-year program to fund other priorities. AA would enable shipyards to do long-range planning, which ought to at least increase stability, if not save money. And MYP would become more attractive, because it has the potential to save money.

Table 4.2

PEO Perspective on AA

Pros	Cons
Stabilizes budget, thus enabling commercial shipyards to do long-range planning	Future changes require congressional approval
Promotes reduction in material and labor costs through MYP	Commercial shipyards may attempt to buy in
Makes MYP more attractive	Still requires termination liability
Makes congressional changes less likely	Requires good-quality year-by-year cost estimates

The PEO's negatives include possible attempts by the shipyard to buy in with a suggested larger purchase. During the Naval Sea Systems Command–sponsored business wargame, the shipbuilder's team suggested that, with AA and MYP, the Navy could buy 15 ships for the price of 12. And termination-liability funding would still be required from the PEO's Office of the Chief of Naval Operations sponsors. Finally, the PEO, along with his shipyard or shipyards, is now required to have a pretty good estimate of year-to-year funding. Once funding is appropriated, any changes to funding would require congressional approval, which entails a long and arduous process.

Navy Leadership

A third viewpoint is that of the Navy. By *Navy* we mean the senior leaders—the Chief of Naval Operations (CNO) and the Secretary. Their likely perspectives are summarized in Table 4.3.

Navy leadership favors AA because it would reduce funding peaks, create an early perceived surplus, and have the potential to save money if coupled with MYP. On the negative side, the use of full funding allows the CNO and the Secretary to revise the future-year plan if necessary. Use of AA would reduce that flexibility because some of the future-year budgets would already be committed. The loss of this flexibility would bother the leadership the most. In the past, Congress has added money to the shipbuilding account. The Navy leaders would be unhappy if AA caused such additions to

Table 4.3

Navy Leadership Perspective on AA

Pros	Cons
Has the potential to save money (with MYP)	Reduces future-year flexibility
Creates a "perceived surplus," which the Navy may attempt to use	Once started, difficult to go back to full funding
Reduces funding peaks for carriers and other large procurement items	Might inhibit Congress from adding low-outlay ships to the budget
Is allowed by OMB	Still requires termination liability
	Not as simple as conventional full funding
	Is not favored by OMB

cease—a real possibility. Finally, AA would commit future CNOs and Secretaries of the Navy to a particular course of action, and that would be of concern to both as well.

Office of the Secretary of Defense

The fourth viewpoint is that of the Office of the Secretary of Defense (OSD). Table 4.4 summarizes this viewpoint.

While OSD has a perspective similar to that of the Navy leadership, it provides a different slant to some of the pros and cons. For example, whereas the Navy would desire to spend the early perceived surplus on shipbuilding, the OSD would look at any monies freed up as an opportunity to pay whatever bills rose to the top of the Secretary of Defense's priority list. OSD would be satisfied with the stability in the SCN budget, as well as with the reduction of peaks and valleys in shipbuilding budgets. OSD also would be concerned with the loss of flexibility and the fact that termination liability would still be necessary.

Table 4.4

OSD Perspective on AA

Pros	Cons
Potential to save money (with MYP)	Reduces future-year flexibility
Creates a "perceived surplus," which OSD may intend to use for other than shipbuilding	Once started, difficult to go back to full funding
Reduces funding peaks for carriers and other large procurement items	Not as simple as conventional full funding
Stabilizes shipbuilding account	Is not favored by OMB
	Still requires money for termination liability

Office of Management and Budget

The Office of Management and Budget has a broader, governmental perspective on AA. Table 4.5 reflects this breadth in its summary.

OMB would appreciate the early perceived surplus inherent in AA, as well as the potential to save money with MYP, the reduction of peaks and valleys in shipbuilding budgets, and the stability AA would

Table 4.5

OMB Perspective on AA

Pros	Cons
Potential to save money (with MYP)	Reduces future-year flexibility
Creates a "perceived surplus," which OMB might desire to use for other than shipbuilding priorities	Once started, difficult to go back to full funding
	Encourages buy in by contractors
Reduces funding peaks for carriers and other large procurement items	Not as simple as conventional full funding
Stabilizes shipbuilding account	Reduces pricing and cost-control discipline by the Navy, DoD, and contractor
	Still requires money for termination liability
	Navy use could encourage other departments to try it

provide. However, it would be concerned that future-year flexibility would be reduced and that the necessary discipline with regard to pricing might be lessened. OMB would also be concerned that other governmental departments with less of a cost-control system than DoD has might be encouraged to fund their large capital purchases through advance appropriations.

Congress

Our final perspective is that of Congress. There are many congressional viewpoints. We limit our comments to the appropriators' viewpoint—that is, the Defense Subcommittee of the House Committee on Appropriations and the Senate Appropriations Committee. In this case, it is understood that one house (Senate) believes that AA is good and the other (House), that it is bad. Table 4.6 presents the pros and cons.

The potential of saving money, buying more ships up front, reducing peaks and valleys, and ensuring stability is what the house that favors AA believes is good about AA. The other house, however, believes that committing future Congresses is not good; that future flexibility is important; that overruns would exacerbate this issue; and, finally, that termination-liability funding is still needed.

Table 4.6

Congressional Perspective on AA

Pros	Cons
Has potential to save money (with MYP)	Reduces future-year flexibility
Creates a "perceived surplus," which Congress may use for anything it deems a priority	Once started, difficult to go back to full funding
	Encourages buy in by contractors
Reduces funding peaks for carriers and other large procurements	Reduces pricing and cost-control discipline by the Navy, DoD, and contractor
Stabilizes shipbuilding account	Still requires money for termination liability
Has potential to buy more ships	Navy use could encourage other departments to try it

Summary

We can summarize the preceding review by abstracting the key effects likely to be considered by each participant and integrating their overall reaction into a projected "yes" or "no" attitude about how AA might influence each attribute. The results are shown in Table 4.7.

Table 4.7

Integrated Assessment of Likely Responses by Different Institutional Players

Whether AA . . .	PEO	Industry	Navy Leadership	OSD	OMB	Congress
Saves money	yes	yes	no	no	no	maybe
Stabilizes shipbuilding budget	yes	yes	yes	yes	yes	yes
Impedes future-year flexibility	yes	yes	yes (not a "plus")	yes	yes	yes
Creates "perceived surplus"	yes	yes	yes	yes	yes	yes
Reduces peaks and valleys	yes	yes	yes	yes	yes	yes
Buys more ships	yes	yes	no	no	no	no
Encourages buy in, reduces discipline	no	no	yes	yes	yes	yes
Requires termination liability	yes	yes	yes	yes	yes	yes
Complicates process	yes	yes	yes	yes	yes	yes

Rather than exhaustively walking through this table, let us review how the Navy leaders might perceive each of the items in the integrated assessment. The Navy leaders would understand that AA does not save money; however, they would also understand that there might be a one-time perceived surplus that, if appropriated by Congress, could be used by the Navy. We have suggested that such a "perceived surplus" should not be used for new shipbuilding but, rather, for items that can be expended in a single year without incurring costs in future years. Examples are SSGN conversion and cruiser conversion for the funding of prior-year shipbuilding bills.

The Navy might perceive that AA stabilizes shipbuilding on the one hand, but, on the other hand, that that stability would limit future leadership in its ability to reduce the future-year shipbuilding accounts. In a similar manner, it might agree that AA reduces budgetary peaks and valleys, as seen earlier in Figure 3.7. It would agree that AA would not enable the Navy to buy more ships, but, as described above, that it could satisfy some near-term conversion and shipbuilding shortfall issues. Finally, it would be concerned that, with its inability to change the future-year program, contractors might feel emboldened to buy in and, therefore, that discipline in the shipbuilding business would be reduced.

Finally, we postulate that there would be more organizations in favor of changing the way shipbuilding is funded than against it. Our assessment is shown in Table 4.8. The Army and Air Force, not mentioned previously, might favor AA being applied to shipbuilding because it would be up to the Secretary of Defense and Congress to determine where the "perceived surplus" might be spent. The contractor and the PEO would be in favor for stability reasons, and Navy

Table 4.8

Summary

In Favor	Against
Contractor	DoD
USA and USAF	OMB
PEO	Congress (House)
Navy leadership	
Congress (Senate)	

leadership would be in favor because of the "perceived surplus." The Senate appropriators would appear to be in favor of AA because it makes better use of appropriated funds by not allowing money to "lie fallow."

DoD would not favor AA because it is concerned with lack of discipline, although some elements of the Office of the Secretary of Defense would like to gain access to the "perceived surplus." OMB would believe this is not a good budgeting procedure, and the House of Representatives, House Appropriations Committee would be concerned with committing future Congresses.

BIBLIOGRAPHY

Birkler, John, John F. Schank, James Chiesa, Giles Smith, Irv Blickstein, Ronald D. Fricker, Jr., and Denis Rushworth, *Options for Funding Aircraft Carriers*, Santa Monica, Calif.: RAND, MR-1526-NAVY, 2002.

Cohen, William S., *Report on Naval Vessel Force Structure Requirements*, Washington, D.C., 2000.

Office of Management and Budget, *Planning, Budgeting, and Acquisition of Capital Assets*, Washington, D.C.: Circular No. A-11, Part 3, revised July 2000.

U.S. Department of Defense, Comptroller, *Financial Management Regulation*, Volume 2A, *Budget Formulation and Presentation*, Washington, D.C., 1993.